Looking After Me

Exercise

Crabtree Publishing Company

www.crabtreebooks.com

Crabtree Publishing Company

www.crabtreebooks.com   1-800-387-7650

Published in Canada
Crabtree Publishing
616 Welland Ave.
St. Catharines, ON
L2M 5V6

Published in the United States
Crabtree Publishing
PMB 59051
350 Fifth Avenue, 59th Floor
New York, New York 10118

Senior editor
Jennifer Schofield

Proofreader
Crystal Sikkens

Designer
Sophie Pelham

Project coordinator
Robert Walker

Digital color
Carl Gordon

Production coordinator
Margaret Amy Salter

Editor
Molly Aloian

Prepress technician
Katherine Berti

Copy editor
Adrianna Morganelli

First published in 2008 by Wayland
338 Euston Road
London NW1 3BH

Wayland Australia
Level 17/207 Kent Street
Sydney NSW 2000

Copyright © Wayland 2008

Wayland is a division of
Hachette Children's Books,
a Hachette Livre UK company.

Printed in Canada/082010/SO20100728

Library and Archives Canada Cataloguing in Publication

Gogerly, Liz
　　Exercise / Liz Gogerly ; illustrator, Mike Gordon.

(Looking after me)
Includes index.
ISBN 978-0-7787-4111-4 (bound).--ISBN 978-0-7787-4118-3 (pbk.)

　　1. Exercise--Juvenile fiction. 2. Health--Juvenile fiction.
I. Gordon, Mike II. Title. III. Series: Gogerly, Liz. Looking after me.

PZ7.G562Ex 2008　　　　j823'.92　　　　C2008-903647-6

Library of Congress Cataloging-in-Publication Data

Gogerly, Liz.
　　Exercise / written by Liz Gogerly ; illustrated by Mike Gordon.
　　　　p. cm. -- (Looking after me)
　　Includes index.
　　ISBN-13: 978-0-7787-4111-4 (reinforced library binding : alk. paper)
　　ISBN-10: 0-7787-4111-7 (reinforced library binding : alk. paper)
　　ISBN-13: 978-0-7787-4118-3 (pbk. : alk. paper)
　　ISBN-10: 0-7787-4118-4 (pbk. : alk. paper)
　　1. Exercise--Juvenile literature. 2. Exercise for children--Juvenile
literature. 3. Physical fitness for children--Juvenile literature. I. Gordon,
Mike, ill. II. Title.
　　QP301.G56 2008
　　612'.044--dc22

　　　　　　　　　　　　　　　2008025344

Looking After Me

Exercise

Written by Liz Gogerly
Illustrated by Mike Gordon

We love playing with our grandma. She's not like any other grandmother. She's fast on her feet.

She's as strong as an ox

and she's
very bendy,
too – just
watch her stretch.

Why is grandma so fit?
What's her secret?

When she was little, they didn't have television, so they did a lot of other things instead.

In those days, children always walked to school. They enjoyed the fresh air and they met their friends along the way.

When Grandma
was at school,
children played
more sports.

At home, there were always jobs to do.

Even though she's older now, Grandma still likes to exercise. She told us that it's important that we exercise, too.

When Grandma came to visit, she said, "Don't be a couch potato. Switch off the TV! Put the video games away!"

Grandma told us that exercise is good for your heart and lungs. It keeps you fit and strong, too.

She said that helping around the house is exercise, too.

It can be a lot of fun

and just as good for you as working out!

Grandma took us
on a scooter ride.

Then we went
swimming.

She was amazing!

That night we felt really tired.

We slept so well.

The next morning, we felt happy and full of energy.

Now we have found
a lot of ways to fit
exercise into our day.

We like to walk, cycle,
or skateboard to school.

At school, we play
games during recess.

Sometimes, after school, we play sports.

Emily is fantastic at gymnastics. She's joined the basketball team and has made a lot of new friends.

Tom is terrific at tennis...

and he's captain of the soccer team.

At other times, we go to the park to play hide-and-seek.

As a treat on the weekend, we go to a gym for kids. It has slides, bouncy castles, trampolines, and ball pools.

We like exercising so much that we've got Mom and Dad doing it, too. Now we go on bike rides together.

Or we go for a walk in the woods.

We've discovered something else...
Exercise doesn't have to feel like exercise.

As long as it's fun, it doesn't matter how you get fit.

NOTES FOR PARENTS AND TEACHERS

SUGGESTIONS FOR READING
LOOKING AFTER ME: EXERCISE
WITH CHILDREN

Exercise is the story of twins, Emily and Tom. With the help of their super-fit grandmother, they discover that you need to exercise to keep fit and healthy. The story begins with a visit from their grandmother. Emily and Tom obviously love her company and enjoy listening to what life was like when she was younger. Most children can identify with this relationship with a grandparent or older relative or family friend. You could ask the children about the older people they know. You could suggest they talk to this person about exercise and keeping fit when they were young. This would be a good way of setting up a discussion comparing ways of keeping fit now and in the past.

Today, lack of exercise is often a result of watching too much television and spending long periods of time on computers and playing video games. Like many children their age, the twins enjoy watching television and playing video games and it is their grandmother who suggests they look for other things to do. This would be a good opportunity to talk to the children about their own daily habits. Do they think they watch too much television? Do they play video games? What kinds of exercise do they do? Which new activities would they like to try? By reading on, and looking closely at the illustrations, children will discover a lot of interesting and possibly new ways of exercising. Did they ever think that cleaning, working in the garden, dancing, or walking were forms of exercise?

The story shows that exercising can be fun and it can bring us many more benefits than just keeping fit. For example, Emily and Tom make more friends when they play team sports, such as basketball and soccer. As captain of the soccer team, Tom will learn leadership skills, too. Can the children think of other benefits from exercising?

LOOKING AFTER ME AND CURRICULUM EXPECTATIONS

The Looking After Me series is designed to teach young readers the importance of personal hygiene, proper nutrition, exercise, and personal safety. This series supports key K-4 health education standards in Canada and the United States, including those outlined by the American Association for Health Education. According to these standards, students will

- Describe relationships between personal health behaviors and individual well being
- Explain how childhood injuries and illnesses can be prevented or treated
- Identify responsible health behaviors
- Identify personal health needs
- Demonstrate strategies to improve or maintain personal health
- Demonstrate ways to avoid and reduce threatening situations

BOOKS TO READ

Walk Like a Bear, Stand Like a Tree, Run Like Wind
Carol Bassett and Clare Amy (Nubod Concepts, 2003)
Little Yoga by Rebecca Whitford (Hutchinson Children's Books, 2005)

ACTIVITY

Exercise Charades

This is a great guessing game that the whole class or a group of children can play. Each child in the group needs to think of a sport or any form of exercise. Then they take turns acting out this activity. The person who guesses correctly becomes the next person to act out their chosen activity.

INDEX